CATERPILLARS

CREEPY CRAWLERS

Lynn Stone

The Rourke Book Co., Inc.
Vero Beach, Florida 32964

PHOTO CREDITS
All photos Lynn M. Stone except page 10 © James P. Rowan

Library of Congress Cataloging-in-Publication Data

Stone, Lynn M.
    Caterpillars / by Lynn Stone.
        p. cm. — (Creepy crawlers)
    Includes index.
    Summary: Briefly describes the life cycle of the caterpillar.
    ISBN 1-55916-163-9
    1. Caterpillars—Juvenile literature.   [1. Caterpillars.]
I. Title II. Series: Stone, Lynn M.   Creepy crawlers.
QL 544.2.S774 1995
595.78'043—dc20   95–18457
                                                               CIP
                                                                AC

Printed in the USA

TABLE OF CONTENTS

CATERPILLARS

Caterpillars are the ugly ducklings of the butterfly family. Just as the ugly duckling grew into a beautiful swan, caterpillars grow into beautiful butterflies and moths.

Butterflies and moths pass through different stages, or forms, on their way toward becoming adults. The caterpillar stage is also called the **larva** (LAR vuh) stage. As caterpillars, they look nothing like adult moths and butterflies.

Although butterflies and moths are fliers, caterpillars are crawlers.

As a larva, this caterpillar looks nothing like the adult polyphemus moth that it will become

WHAT CATERPILLARS LOOK LIKE

All caterpillars are soft, wormlike creatures. Some caterpillars, however, are tiny and others are finger-length.

Many caterpillars are brightly colored. Most have smooth skins, but others are nearly covered by spines or hairy bristles, like a toothbrush. The biggest, brightest, most bristly caterpillars look quite fearsome!

Most caterpillars have three pairs of clawed legs. They also have two to five pairs of knobby **prolegs** (PRO legz) to help them crawl.

The stinging spines of a saddleback caterpillar disappear when it becomes an adult moth

KINDS OF CATERPILLARS

Scientists have found about 100,000 **species** (SPEE sheez), or kinds, of butterflies and moths. That means 100,000 different kinds of caterpillars!

Some caterpillars are called worms. Tent worms, meal worms, silkworms, and tomato worms, for example, are actually caterpillars. These "worms" grow up to be moths. Real worms remain worms throughout their lives.

One hairy American caterpillar is called a "woolly bear." This "bear" grows up to be an isabella moth.

The woolly bear caterpillar is the larva stage of an isabella moth

WHAT CATERPILLARS EAT

Almost all caterpillars eat plants. Caterpillars have mouth parts to chew leaves and other plant parts. A few species chew their way into fruits, leaves, or stems and live within a plant.

Predators (PRED uh terz) are the animals that hunt other animals for food. Many birds and tiny wasps and flies are predators of caterpillars.

Caterpillars scare some predators away with their stinging bristles and bad scent. A few caterpillars have large spots that look like eyes. These make-believe eyes may frighten predators, too.

The "eye spots" on some caterpillars, like those on this pandora sphinx, may frighten predators

A cecropia moth caterpillar chomps its way through leaves before resting in the pupal, or cocoon stage

The chrysalises of three butterflies are attached to a leaf in a Costa Rican rain forest

HOW CATERPILLARS LIVE

Moth caterpillars spin long, fine threads of silk from their mouths. They use the silk to help build shelters called **cocoons** (kuh KOONZ). Caterpillars in the cocoons change into adult moths.

Most butterfly caterpillars create a resting shelter called a **chrysalis** (KRIHS uh lis). The caterpillar becomes an adult butterfly inside the shiny, crisp chrysalis.

Caterpillars usually live and feed alone. A few species, such as the tent caterpillars, feed together.

A cecropia moth caterpillar spun this cocoon of silk

FROM EGG TO ADULT

Adult moths and butterflies lay eggs, usually on a plant that the larvas will eat. Caterpillars—the larvas—hatch from eggs, the first stage of their lives. The caterpillar is the second stage.

The cocoon or chrysalis is the third and **pupal** (PU pul) stage. The adult moth or butterfly that leaves the pupal shelter has reached the fourth and final stage of life.

Some species make the journey from egg to adult in 30 days. Other species take several months or years.

A cecropia moth lays its eggs

RELATIVES

Moths and butterflies are insects. Like other insects, they are boneless animals with six legs and three distinct body sections—head, **thorax** (THOR ax), and **abdomen** (AB do men).

Most butterflies fly by day and have club-shaped antennas. Moths are generally night fliers with "furry" bodies and "feathery" antennas.

The closest relatives of moths and butterflies are some of the other insects—caddis flies, wasps, ants, and bees.

Luna has the "feathery" antennas and "furry" body of most moths

GROWING UP

A caterpillar fattens up as it eats. Trouble is, the caterpillar's skin doesn't grow with its body. The skin won't even stretch.

A caterpillar solves this problem by growing a new skin under the old. The old skin finally becomes so tight it splits. The caterpillar—in its new skin—crawls out of the old.

The change of skins is called a molt. A caterpillar usually undergoes four or five molts before spinning a shelter.

After molting, these tiny cecropia moth caterpillars will have new skins and brighter colors (see page 12)

CATERPILLARS AND PEOPLE

The silkworm caterpillar is so valuable it's raised on silk farms, especially in China. A silkworm can spin a thread of silk three-quarters of a mile long!

Certain kinds of caterpillars are pests. They eat corn, tomatoes, the leaves of entire forests, and even clothing.

Some of the spiny caterpillars, like the saddleback, should not be touched. Their spines can irritate skin.

Many caterpillars should be left alone for another reason: Sixteen kinds of American butterflies and moths are in danger of disappearing forever.

Glossary

abdomen (AB do men) — the third and rearmost part of the three main body parts of an insect

chrysalis (KRIHS uh lis) — the pupa, or resting, stage of a butterfly; the pupa's outer covering

cocoon (kuh KOON) — the silk covering that moths spin around themselves for protection during their pupal, or resting stage

larva (LAR vuh) — the stage of development between egg and pupa or egg and adult in certain animals, such as insects

predators (PRED uh terz) — animals that hunt other animals for food

prolegs (PRO legz) — the fleshy, leglike knobs on the abdomen of some insect larvas, such as caterpillars

pupal (PU pul) — referring to the pupa, or resting stage of a butterfly or moth

species (SPEE sheez) — within a group of closely related animals, one certain kind, such as a *monarch* butterfly

thorax (THOR ax) — the middle part of the three main body parts of insects, between the head and the abdomen

INDEX